BRITAIN IN OLD PHOTOGRAPHS

# OXFORDSHIRE AT PLAY

MALCOLM GRAHAM

SUTTON PUBLISHING LIMITED

OXFORDSHIRE BOOKS

Sutton Publishing Limited
Phoenix Mill · Thrupp · Stroud
Gloucestershire · GL5 2BU

First published 1997



Cover photographs: *front*: Cyclists on the Wantage road, 1898; *back*: Folk dancing in Thame, 1950s.

Title page photograph: A boy buys ice cream from a stall in Banbury Market Place, 1908.

**British Library Cataloguing in Publication Data**
A catalogue record for this book is available from the British Library.

ISBN 0-7509-1676-1

Typeset in 10/12 Perpetua.
Typesetting and origination by
Sutton Publishing Limited.
Printed in Great Britain by
Ebenezer Baylis, Worcester.

Edward, Prince of Wales, the future Edward VIII, goes for a drive with some of his friends while at Magdalen College in 1912.

# CONTENTS

Shenington football team in its club colours in 1876. This remarkably early photograph of a village football team includes the Revd Arthur Blythman, Rector of Shenington (standing at the back), who was probably its founder.

Motorcyclists prepare for a race in the Banbury area in about 1910.

# INTRODUCTION

'All work and no play makes Jack a dull boy.' The old saying emphasises the crucial importance of leisure time as a chance to unwind and recharge the mental batteries. Early commercial photographers were quick to recognise that pictures of people enjoying themselves would find a ready market; at the same time, men and women who could afford to do so were keen to commission photographs of important events in their lives, souvenirs of happy moments that they would treasure for the rest of their lives. As the technology of photography developed and became more accessible, it became easier for individuals to record a whole range of events and experiences for their family albums. Many thousands of these recreational images, from both commercial and private sources, are now in Oxfordshire's public collections and this selection of photographs helps to show how much or, in some cases, how little our leisure interests have changed since Victorian times.

*Home and Family*, the focus of so much of our leisure time, forms the theme for the first section. Recreational opportunities were always plentiful in Oxfordshire's grander houses, but were few and far between in crowded or insanitary homes. In St Thomas', Oxford, in the mid-nineteenth century, frustrated gardeners grew plants in old pots and pans in a bid to cheer up gloomy courts and yards. From Victorian times, most new properties provided some space for children's games or personal hobbies and they generally had gardens where adults could grow flowers or vegetables and where young and old alike could eat, relax or play. Pets could be accommodated in these roomier houses and there was generally somewhere to store bicycles, which could be used for country outings as well as for getting to work. Better-off families might enjoy regular seaside holidays and, for them, cars soon increased the range of their outings and the luxuriousness of their picnics. These households were also quick to experiment with the new home entertainments which only gradually filtered down to ordinary folk.

Beyond family life, there were increasing recreational opportunities *Out and About*. Children and adults could still have fun lounging about on street corners or take advantage of sudden floods or freeze-ups, but local councils or other bodies were also beginning to provide formal recreation grounds. Travel beyond the locality became easier because of excursion trains, Thames steamers and, eventually, charabancs or motor coaches. Such delights were beyond the means of many people but they became more generally accessible through the annual outings arranged by employers, church and other social organisations. These excursions were a break from routine, but were sometimes memorable for all the wrong reasons; in August 1870, for example, Oxford City Police excursionists must have been thankful to get back home after their river trip to Nuneham was ruined by heavy and persistent rain. Many people had more time for leisure pursuits because of a gradual reduction in the length of the working day and the introduction of early closing days by larger shops. Bank Holidays were introduced in 1871, adding a new dimension to many lives; locally, Uffington Castle seems to have become a particularly attractive destination on August Bank Holidays. Like-minded individuals banded together in clubs and societies to pursue common interests such as archaeology and publications such as Henry Taunt's *A new map of the River Thames* (1872) encouraged people to explore their surroundings.

*Traditional Customs* continued to provide a means of letting off steam, but the authorities were increasingly keen to refine them and moderate some of their wilder excesses. Fairs provided an annual bacchanalia in many Oxfordshire communities and, in Oxford, St Giles's Fair grew massively in Victorian times as special trains brought visitors from as far afield as Wolverhampton and Cardiff. In the mid-Victorian years, the fair included large drinking saloons and contemporaries were outraged by immorality in nearby streets and in the Parks. Stricter licensing controls and more effective policing reduced drunkenness at the fair and the creation of the University Parks in 1864–6 denied the amorously inclined easy access to open space. Fairgoers also faced a direct challenge from evangelists such as the Revd Henry Bazely whose Bible Stall was an annual incitement to good behaviour. Attempts were made to ban St Giles' Fair but the police eventually accepted that, in its less rowdy form, it served as a safety valve for boisterous youngsters. If fairs became more civilised, May Day customs were also recast in a more respectable guise. The May Morning ceremony on Magdalen Tower, where choristers had formerly thrown rotten eggs at the spectators, was made more orderly and reverent by the Revd J.R. Bloxam, Fellow of Magdalen, in 1844. In rural areas, May garlanding ceased to be a licence for children to play truant from school and it was organised instead by church, school or large house as a picturesque occasion. The beating of Oxford City and parish boundaries resumed as part of a growing interest in old customs and the Headington Quarry Morris Dancers were persuaded out of retirement for a public performance at Oxford's Corn Exchange in March 1899. Morris Dancing soon became popular again among both participants and spectators.

*Special Events* offered further scope for enjoyment. Fairs and Club Days were annual, long-awaited events in many towns and villages but an increasing number of carnivals, fêtes and shows began to challenge the primacy of these traditional amusements. Some of these events became annual fixtures in their own right, not only providing fun and games for the community but also raising money for the local hospital or some other good cause. National events and priorities made their presence felt in the annual celebration of Empire Day and in the Victory celebrations at the end of both world wars. Local communities were also reminded of the changing world by such excitements as the sudden unplanned arrival of an aeroplane or the recording of a wireless programme.

Towns and villages alike were always keen to celebrate *Royal Occasions*. Royal visits provided long-awaited moments of excitement and even the prospect of royalty passing through could draw crowds; at Wantage, for example, thousands of people gathered in the Market Place on 13 June 1898 for a brief view of the Prince and Princess of Wales on their way from Lockinge House to Wantage Road railway station. Jubilees and Coronations were marked by ox roasts, fancy dress processions, parties for the children and huge public dinners. Abingdon organised water sports which included a challenging race in round tubs; the accompanying land sports featured a washing competition which was only open to women. The town also celebrated royal occasions by the quaint custom of throwing buns from County Hall; at the time of Edward VII's Coronation in 1902 one well-thrown bun hit the veranda of the Queen's Hotel on the opposite side of the Market Place! Local newspapers commented at length on the patriotic decoration of business premises and private houses and the centre of Henley, for instance, positively bristled with flags and bunting during George V's Silver Jubilee in 1935.

Much recreation, particularly for men, continued to be focused upon *Pubs*. Thirsty men have always looked to their local pub for one or more refreshing pints during or after the working day. The pub was also a meeting place away from a home which might be crowded or lacking in creature comforts. Landlords often ran social clubs for regulars and organised annual outings which typically stopped at one pub on the way to another! The increasing number of pleasure boats on the Thames brought a different clientele to riverside pubs and the King's Arms at Sandford was quick to cater for the 'river tourist'. On land, too, the bicycle was bringing the newly mobile townsman to country pubs by the turn of the century; between the wars, motor cars continued this trend, often bringing back to life roadside pubs and hotels which had lost virtually all their passing trade when the railways came.

Away from the public house, *Recreation* opportunities were becoming much more varied. Making music, whether at home or in local bands, became more popular, partly because musical instruments and sheet music became cheaper and more readily available. Keen actors could be found in large households and country villages as well as in towns and there was great enthusiasm for historical pageants in the first half of the twentieth century. Colossal circuses were major attractions in Victorian times and moving pictures burst on to the scene in the late 1890s, appearing first at fairgrounds and other temporary venues before permanent cinemas were built. Bingo became so popular in the 1950s and 1960s that cinemas like the Grand in Banbury and the Regal in Oxford were converted into bingo halls. At the same time, traditional ballroom dancing was largely ousted by rock 'n' roll and other modern dances.

*Sport* provided a leisure time interest for growing numbers of people. The traditional field sports of hunting, shooting and fishing continued to be popular, but the Victorian period saw the development of a whole range of team and individual sports. Some of this sporting activity continued to be based in pubs, but many churchmen were keen to encourage team games on the public school and university model as a way of encouraging 'rational recreation' and stressing the relevance of church or chapel in the wider community; large employers such as Morris Motors and Pressed Steel were equally keen to reinforce loyalty to the company by providing good sporting and other leisure facilities. The development of rowing was furthered by the prominence of Varsity rowing and the success of the Henley Regatta, which became Royal through the patronage of Prince Albert from 1851. Individuals banded together to form sporting clubs and then worked towards providing the facilities that they needed; at the same time, inter-club competition was made easier by increasing leisure time and swifter travel. The development of racing cycles, motorcycles and gliders provided new sporting challenges and the brief fashion for roller skating in about 1910 was arguably the first twentieth-century athletic craze. Tennis was thought graceful enough for the Victorian lady and some women, suitably attired in long dresses, played cricket at the White House ground in Oxford in 1891 'without the least hint of indecency'. A massive petition from 1,707 women (and 10 men) was required in 1900 before Oxford City Council would agree to provide a women's bathing place at Long Bridges. Only very gradually did women achieve equal access to many of the sporting facilities which men took for granted.

*Varsity Life* offered a bewildering range of leisure opportunities to undergraduates and plenty of entertainment for other Oxonians and visitors. Sport figured high on the agenda of many students whether that meant rowing, athletics or following one of the local hunts. There was ample time for a bit of fun during Rag Weeks or fancy dress parties and Oxford provided many delightful venues for balls, dinners, tea parties, river trips or simply snoozing in the sun. Eights Week and many of the events of Commemoration Week attracted large numbers of visitors to Oxford, but the Victorian University was already beginning to encourage adult education and to attract the first conferences during vacations. The University's wider educational role was also evident in the archaeological excavations on the line of the city wall which brought an interesting aspect of Oxford's history to general notice in 1899. The concept of life-long learning would, however, have been a source of great alarm to an undergraduate like C.F. Cholmondeley, who recorded in his diary for 20 April 1885:

'Fine day. I went up to our cricket ground and had some cricket practice, but did not get any of the professional's bowling. I went to be photographed by Hill and Saunders in a studious position to make Papa think I work.'

# ACKNOWLEDGEMENTS

Most of the photographs in this book are from the Oxfordshire Photographic Archive and Oxfordshire County Council's partnership museums at Abingdon, Banbury and Wantage. I am greatly indebted to my colleague, Nuala la Vertue, for helping to find many excellent and formerly unpublished photographs. I would also like to thank Howard Fuller for giving me access to images housed at the Vale and Downland Museum in Wantage.

I am very grateful to the following for permission to reproduce their photographs:
Laszlo Grof (p. 21 upper, p. 23 both)
Angela Spencer-Harper (p. 105 lower)
Tom Worley (p. 63 upper, p. 108 lower)

SECTION ONE

# HOME & FAMILY

*Relaxing decorously in the gardens of Ditchley Park in about 1880. Tending these immaculate flower beds would have required a small army of gardeners, but their work had to be slotted in around the recreational needs of the Dillon family.*

The Cheesman family photographed in their garden at Caldecote Farm, Caulcott, near Lower Heyford, in August 1897. Members of the family were farmers here for several generations.

Cyclists enjoy exclusive possession of the Wantage road in August 1898. They were members of the Barrett family on a country outing from their home in St Margaret's Road, North Oxford.

Bare feet contrast with formal clothes as the Barretts risk putting their toes in the sea at Margate in July 1898. Behind them the crowded beach is studded with parasols and the promenade is lined with other visitors.

A break from tennis for the Turrill sisters and their friends in the garden of Fern Cottage at Garsington in the 1890s.

Hemmed in by dolls, a wooden horse and other playthings, Madge Reeves plays happily in a world of her own at the family home in Henley in about 1899.

The Webb family in their garden in about 1900. This delightful group, photographed in the Oxford area by Henry Taunt, features the children's favourite toys, including a rocking horse and a cart bearing the family's name.

The Oliver family at Stonesfield comes together for a Golden Wedding in about 1900. The group includes Mr and Mrs Austin, seated on the right with their infant daughter Maud; their son Ernest is in front of Mrs Austin.

Wearing a sailor suit and an extraordinary hat, one of the little Morrell boys sits warily on a horse at Headington Hill Hall in about 1900. The horse looks very docile but the bowler-hatted man, presumably a groom, was there to ensure that no accident took place.

The members of an exclusive weekend house party at Broughton Castle in 1901. The group includes Edward VII (seated centre), the Portuguese Ambassador, Marques de Soveral (seated right) and Baron Ferdinand de Rothschild (back row, sixth from left).

Tending the garden in about 1900: Emily Margetts of Watlington prepares to mow the lawn while her husband potters in the background.

A picnic at Appleton Manor in 1903 when youngsters were able to sprawl on the grass while the adults sat politely beside outdoor tables.

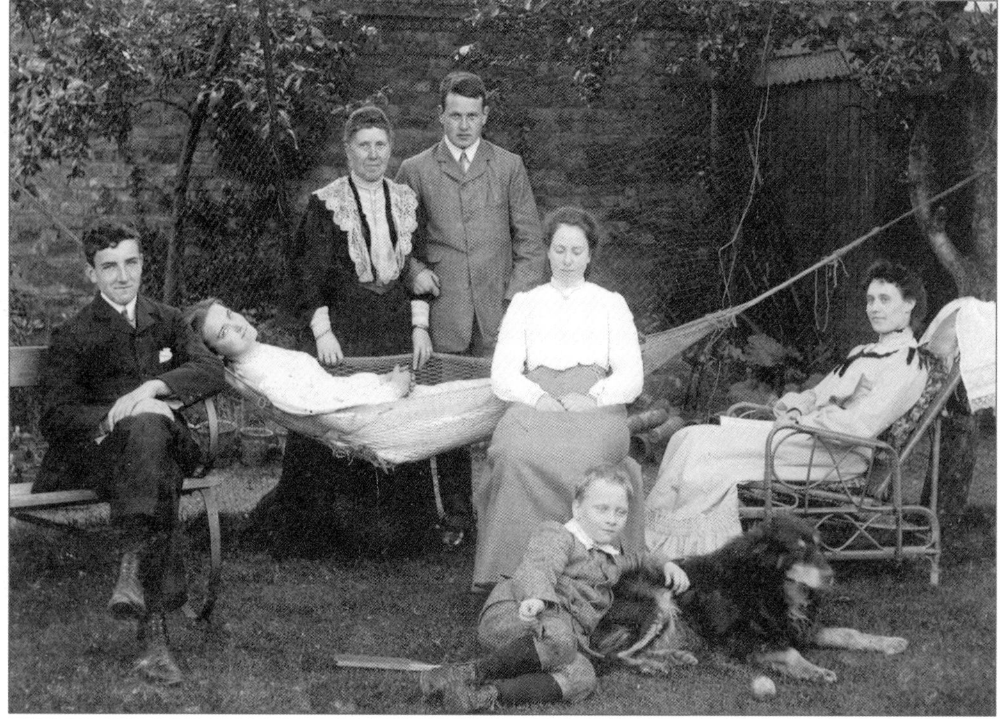

The members of an extended Oxford family relax in their garden with their pet dog in the 1900s. The view encapsulates the attraction of the private garden as a retreat from the pressures of the world.

Anyone for tennis? Members of the Clare family pose proudly with their racquets at Clanfield in the 1900s.

First steps: Gladys Neal is helped along Mill Road, Shiplake, by Mabel (left) and Olive in about 1908.

Relaxing by the fish tank: William Henry Axtell, the Oxford stonemason, sits comfortably in a corner of his garden at 123 Iffley Road in about 1910.

Afternoon tea in the back garden of a house in Divinity Road, Oxford, in about 1910. Even a small garden provided the opportunity for outdoor meals and storage space for the bicycle, which could be ridden for pleasure as well as business.

Charles Robertson with his wife, family and servants in the grounds of Apsley Paddox in Banbury Road, Oxford, in the summer of 1913. The Robertsons had extensively remodelled the house and garden since 1911 and this photograph was one of several taken to celebrate the completion of that work.

One for the family album: Alice, wife of Frank Packer, the Chipping Norton photographer, with her children, Basil and Gwennie, pictured on their Thursday afternoon constitutional walk on 29 June 1913.

Basil and Gwennie Packer hold on happily to a giant Christmas cracker in front of one of their father's photographic studio backdrops at 28 High Street, Chipping Norton, in about 1913.

Watched by two fashionably dressed ladies, children at play seem all set for a motoring expedition from Oakley Road, Chinnor, in about 1914. Douglas Sharp is the boy with the rug over his knees and the baby in the back is Rowland Hill.

All eyes focus on George Mark Morrell and his bride, Edith, after their wedding at South Stoke on 6 June 1918. Edith was the daughter of the Revd Hubert Nind, vicar of South Stoke.

Harry Payne, a tobacconist in Cowley Road, Oxford, keeps up appearances as he paddles with his wife and family during a seaside holiday in about 1920.

A very young Cowley motorist in the 1920s: Aileen Middleton, the proud possessor of this pedal car, seems understandably reluctant to keep still instead of careering round the garden at 67 Hollow Way.

Enjoying early wireless transmissions in the garden of Chinnor post office in the 1920s. The listeners, from left to right, were Rowland Hill, Douglas Sharp, ? Blackburn and Rowland's mother, Mrs Hill.

Happy picnickers relax on Chinnor Hill in the 1920s. The smiling trio were, from left to right, Betty Hillhouse, the daughter of a Commander in the United States Navy, Douglas Sharp and Mrs Hill.

A Shiplake family goes to the beach: Gladys Neal with Olive, Billy and Tommy enjoying themselves at Hayling Island in July 1936.

A cheerful wedding group at Chalgrove church on 27 September 1947 when Kenneth Tuckwell married Mary Franklin. Max Tuckwell was the best man and the senior bridesmaids were Sylvia Nash and Margaret Hook; the little bridesmaid in front of the happy couple is thought to have been Diana Keane.

*SECTION TWO*

# OUT & ABOUT

*The Oxford photographer, Henry Taunt, and his two assistants relax beside their camping skiff in about 1878. A bunch of carrots dangles from the mast and, hidden away in the deepest recesses of the boat, straw mattresses promise a fitful night's sleep.*

Picnicking in style: an exclusive boating party settles in beside the Thames at Hart's Wood near Goring in about 1880.

Visitors on the Chinese Bridge at Nuneham Courtenay in about 1880. The Harcourt family opened Nuneham Park to the public on a regular basis from the early nineteenth century and, until the 1930s, it was virtually an inland seaside resort and the destination of many local outings.

Entertainment at Headington Hill Hall for the families of Morrell's Brewery employees, perhaps in July 1903. This party was probably held to celebrate James Herbert Morrell's twenty-first birthday and hats seem to have been compulsory for all ages.

'Queen Anne tombs and their admirers': the original caption to a photograph which shows historians on an Architectural Association excursion making a close study of the tombstones in Alkerton churchyard in 1885.

Waiting for something exciting to happen: loungers at the junction of Cornmarket and Gloucester Street in Faringdon in about 1895.

Watched by the rest of his party, a man burrows enthusiastically into the earthen ramparts of Uffington Castle to try to uncover their secrets on August Bank Holiday in 1900.

An informal moment during the Bicester Methodist Sunday School's outing in about 1900. Such outings were usually a reward for good attendance and impeccable behaviour during the year.

Washing-up neatly stacked and the broom set aside: campers at Bablockhythe enjoy a period of relaxation beside their tent in about 1900.

Three little girls sit beside the base of the thirteenth-century cross at Wood Eaton in March 1902. The girl at the top was Kathleen Gird.

Boys jousting with mops at the Oxford Band of Hope picnic in July 1902. The event was held in Alderman Saunders' field and included a massive tea for both the victors and the vanquished.

Squaring the circle: two elegant Edwardian ladies study the guide book at the Rollright Stones in 1904.

W.R. Morris takes his wife, Lilian, and some friends for a spin on the Garsington road in 1911. Within a few years he would be able to make similar outings in Morris cars.

Two oarswomen guide their craft beside St Helen's Wharf in Abingdon in about 1910. A notice in front of the Old Anchor Inn invites travellers to use the adjoining landing stage for all hotels and the Great Western Railway.

Colonel Henry Goode shows off his steam launch 'Coronation' on the Thames at Sutton Courtenay in 1911. Launches provided a new way of exploring the river but they were deplored by many traditionalists.

Children playing 'ducks and drakes' at the sheep washing place in Barracks Lane, Cowley, in July 1914. In the background, golfers are making their way to the nearby golf course which had opened in 1875.

Reluctance to travel at Abingdon in about 1918, when the children who are going nowhere manage to look much happier than the employees of Clark's Clothing Factory whose annual works outing is about to begin.

Dorchester families at the seaside in the late 1920s. Their clothing suggests that the weather was far from perfect, but they look determined to enjoy themselves on this annual day out.

An instrument of punishment becomes an object of fun: two children at Great Tew clamber on the old village stocks in March 1929.

Winter sports at Chipping Norton in February 1929, when heavy snow created ideal conditions for sledging in steep streets like The Leys.

A Morris Minor provides easy access to the Oxfordshire countryside for these blackberry pickers in 1930.

Children enjoying themselves at Chipping Norton recreation ground between the wars. A boy is speeding down the tall slide, menaced perhaps by his brother at the bottom but threatening in his turn the girls who are playing in the deceleration area.

Taking a break from work; women employees of Charles Early & Co. Ltd, the Witney blanket makers, relax by the River Windrush during their lunch hour one summer's day in 1947.

Flooding can be fun as Oxford City's goalkeeper, A. Jefferson, paddles a friend past the Duke of Monmouth pub in Abingdon Road, Oxford, on 17 March 1947.

French visitors to Chipping Norton pose on their bikes in the Market Square in April 1949. Behind them and nearer the Town Hall, wartime blackout paint is still evident in front of the road sign.

The seaside comes to Cardigan Street in Jericho, Oxford, in June 1955. Children plough happily through the floods while returning from school; more surprisingly perhaps, their mums were also putting a brave face on things.

Walking on the water at Eynsham: a Polish man uses self-propelled water skis to make a remarkable journey down the Thames in the 1950s.

All smiles at Sandford Lock in June 1957. These travellers from the London area were on a Townswomen's Guild excursion, which included this trip on a Salter's steamer and a visit to Blenheim Palace.

Enthusiastic young trainspotters on the platform at Oxford station in May 1958. The locomotive beside them was *Lady Margaret Hall*, which appropriately spent most of its working life at Oxford.

*SECTION THREE*

# CUSTOMS

*Preceded by a giant civic flag, beaters of Oxford's boundaries march across Port Meadow towards the ditch marking the disputed boundary with Wolvercote Common in 1892. Some villagers, led by the local vicar, the Revd F.W. Langton, were waiting for them and there was a brief Battle of Wolvercote before the City mace and flag could be planted across the ditch.*

Burford Hiring Fair in about 1895, looking down the High Street from the corner of Witney Street. Held in the autumn, hiring fairs enabled farmworkers and others to seek employment for the new farming year, but they also provided all the traditional fairground amusements.

A coconut shy, swings and other amusements on offer at Bampton in August 1904. This pleasure fair, justifying the high-level sign for 'Robinson Cheap Butcher', provided entertainment for folk attending the horse fair held nearby.

Well wrapped-up Great Rollright children with their May Garland, complete with doll, on May morning in 1907.

Beating the bounds of the parish of St Peter in the East and St Cross in Longwall Street, Oxford, in May 1907. At this point, the beaters were using scaling ladders to climb the fifteenth-century perimeter wall of Magdalen College.

Crowds parade along St Giles' during the fair in September 1907. On the left, the taximen's shelter had been commandeered as a temporary police station in the annual battle against pickpockets and troublemakers.

Crowds on Magdalen Bridge strain to hear the choristers of Magdalen College sing the *Hymnus Eucharisticus* on 1 May 1908. The occasion looks very respectable but contemporaries complained about children who blew May horns made of willow to disturb the May morning tranquillity.

The employees of Ball & Son's New Lyceum try to drum up trade at Banbury Fair in the 1900s. The Lyceum offered 'Only one class of pictures: the Best' and promised seating accommodation for all classes at a charge of 3*d* for adults and 2*d* for children.

Children with May garlands outside the village school in Iffley in the 1900s. This was a respectable recasting of an old May Day custom which led to many unauthorised absences from Victorian country schools.

May festival celebrations at Hornton in 1908 which were organised by the Primitive Methodist Sunday School. This photograph was taken on the village green by Mr Wheeler of Banbury, and the children's banner probably read 'Welcome Miss Stanley'; Miss D. Stanley was the May Queen.

Kirtlington folk ride on a roundabout and enjoy the sights and sounds of the fairground in the 1900s. This fair, held among the elms on the village green, traditionally accompanied the village Club Day.

Galloping horses are replaced by new-fangled cars on a roundabout at the Michaelmas Fair in Banbury Market Place in 1910.

Smiles are mixed with frowns of concentration as stick dancers struggle to hold their positions for the photographer at Abingdon's Revels on 14 July 1913.

Ready to dance: Steeple Aston's Morris Dancers and an interested observer in 1920.

Headington Quarry Morris dancers at the Six Bells pub on Whit Monday 1914. The dancers, from left to right, are Teddy Hooper, 'Todge' Smith, Harry 'Murderer' Green, -?- , 'Shingle' Smith, William Kimber, ? Hooper and Sam Smith.

Muted pleasure as a sidesaddle rider experiences Mrs Bird's gallopers at St Giles' Fair in the 1920s. Steam-powered roundabouts and other rides were a feature of the fair from the 1870s and gallopers still enjoy pride of place near the Martyrs' Memorial today.

A new use for truncheons: the Oxford City Police Morris Dancing side in 1925. In the back row, from left to right, are B. Jefford, S. Waters, H. Cox, H. Parker, H. Pyke, F. Carter, W. Edgington; in the front row, H. Brookland, B. Fennell, Chief Constable C.R. Fox, J. Hewett and their instructor, William Kimber.

Gallopers and swingboats fill Ock Street in Abingdon during the Michaelmas fair in October 1934. The picture was taken from the top of a helter-skelter and looks east past Hemmings Bros, cycle repairers, at no. 123 on the left, and the Cross Keys pub on the right.

Spectators enjoying the May Day festivities at Over Norton in 1937.

The May Queen and her Maids of Honour opposite the church at Hook Norton in 1938. On the far side of the road a little boy seems more interested in trying to toss the caber with a telegraph pole.

Waving to mum and dad from the swingboats at Abingdon in October 1952.

Free expression folk dancing in Upper High Street, Thame, in the 1950s. Two Morris dancers have joined in while others wait their turn; William Kimber, the famous fiddler of the Headington Morris side, is seated near the band wearing a dark jacket and cap.

Oxford University Morris Dancers stepping it out at Kirtlington in the 1970s during the village Lamb Ale celebrations.

*SECTION FOUR*

# SPECIAL EVENTS

*James Porter, a livery stable keeper in St Aldate's, Oxford, risks taking a coach and four on to the frozen Thames on 19 January 1891. Hauled by specially shod horses, the coach made two journeys between the University Barge and Long Bridges, entertaining hundreds of sightseers in the process.*

Crowds enjoying a garden fête at Lockinge House, the home of Lord and Lady Wantage, in about 1900. Many social events were held in these extensive grounds, including notably the Lockinge Revels of 1885, which were an attempt to revive the pageants of the Elizabethan era.

No shortage of potential diners for the Headington Quarry sheep roast in 1900. This event seems to have been an annual feature in the Quarry at the turn of the century.

'Tilting the bucket': no doubt to the delight of the crowd, a brave victim receives a soaking at the Henley Liberal Fête in 1900.

A banner proclaiming 'God Save The King' and another one depicting Edward VII are just two of the patriotic symbols evident in this Empire Day group at Adderbury on 24 May 1905.

Living Bridge in the grounds of Faringdon House during the town's Flower Show in July 1906. In the distance nearer the parish church keen tennis players ignore the distraction and get on with their game.

The crowd around the hoop-la stall at Sibford Fête on 10 August 1909. A notice on the stall announces 'The new game of hoop-la. 2 rings 1*d*. All You Ring You Have.'

Entrants for the costume race perch on and in front of an Oxfordshire waggon at the Mollington Fête in August 1910.

The Oxford horse tram service across Magdalen Bridge is interrupted in about 1910 as an elaborate parade led by the Ancient Order of Foresters' float causes people to spill out on to the roadway.

One of the events holds the concentration of most of the spectators at Bicester Horse Show in 1910.

Cropredy fête in June 1910 with a be-hatted crowd leaning over hurdles and awaiting the next event. In the background, an elaborate 'Cokernut' shy is trumpeted as the 'Excelsior Throwing Saloon', where all patrons are promised fair play.

Club Day procession through Clanfield in about 1911, when the band was preceded by a man bearing a huge Union Jack. Village clubs were local savings groups which enabled people to put a little money aside each week in readiness for the proverbial rainy day.

A crowd gathers excitedly around the Avro aeroplane, which was the first plane to land in Abingdon when it came down in a field off the Culham road on 13 January 1912. The pilot had been flying from Brooklands to Oxford, but ran short of oil because fog had forced him to follow the meandering course of the Thames.

A bizarre crowd of pierrots, men in fancy dress and uniformed soldiers pose for the photographer before a comic football match held as part of the Wantage Peace celebrations in 1919. Frank Woolford was the man in the top hat in the front row and Nobby Chapman was the pierrot seated on the right.

A boy lounges against his bike, distracted from whatever he was doing by a carnival procession through Queen Street, Eynsham, in the 1920s.

Shopping Week in Banbury in 1922, and sightseers are attracted by a band and the unlikely prospect of girls maypole dancing on a horse-drawn waggon. The delivery vans parked beside the pavement were probably due to join the procession in a few moments.

Dog handlers control their Pekingese on a trestle table while waiting for the judges at Thame Show on 20 September 1928. This was just one tiny corner of a dog show that included over 1,400 entries.

Children mount a spirited Empire Day tableau outside the parish church at Churchill in May 1928. Placards proudly announce that the Empire includes Newfoundland, West Africa, Australia, New Zealand and Jamaica; behind the pram, children exhort everyone to 'Buy British Empire Goods'.

Some of the cloche-hatted ladies manage a smile in this view of spectators at Charlbury's British Legion Fête in about 1930. The child in the push-chair looks unamused and ready for a new diversion.

If the drinks were genuine, there would have been no shortage of volunteers for this Witney Carnival float in 1931. The men in the mobile thatched 'pub' were promoting the products of Clinch & Co., the local brewers.

The rain does nothing to diminish the pleasure of Mabel Baggerley, Wantage Carnival Queen, during speeches in the Market Square in 1936.

Local families pose outside Heythrop House in 1937 with some of the Jesuit priests who had invited them to come for tea. Heythrop was owned by the Jesuits between 1923 and 1969.

The top table requires some reorganising before the speeches at Chipping Norton's National Children's Home and Orphanage Fête in 1937. The sound system for the event was provided by the Wallingford wireless engineer, John K. Hoddinott, and the firm's van can be seen in the background.

Children in fancy dress teeter on the kerb during a Horton Hospital fund-raising event in 1937, when a carnival procession toured Banbury.

The Wootton and Glympton Group that featured in episode six of the Blenheim and Woodstock Pageant, which was held in Blenheim Park on 1 and 2 August 1938. The production, involving no fewer than 600 performers, covered English history from King Alfred to the Duke of Marlborough.

Local residents come out in force to mark VE (Victory in Europe) Day with a tea party in Wellington Square, Oxford, in May 1945. The four soldiers turning round to look at the photographer had simply been walking past and were happy to join in the fun.

A beer barrel takes pride of place at the front of the group as Salford villagers celebrate VJ (Victory in Japan) Day outside the Black Horse on 15 August 1945.

'Give her the money, Mabel!' Contestants on stage in Chipping Norton in the 1950s during a recording of the BBC's long-running programme, *Have a Go*, which was introduced by Wilfrid Pickles.

A model appears on the catwalk from a giant mock-up of a television set during the Co-operative Fashion Show in Chipping Norton Town Hall in the 1950s. The audience seems to have been entirely female, apart from one man seated close to the Emergency Exit.

A chilly wind billows round Lewis Penney's float as models demonstrate Aristoc fashions during a Wantage Carnival in the mid-1950s. Lewis Penney's were drapers and outfitters in Wantage Market Place.

A problem for the judges at Chipping Norton in the 1970s when the entries for the children's fancy dress competition included a yokel, a knight, an astronaut, an archer and an extraordinary bird with a flower pot for a head.

*SECTION FIVE*

# ROYAL OCCASIONS

*Crowds line Broad Street, Oxford, and fill every available window and balcony as Edward, Prince of Wales, lays the foundation stone of the Indian Institute on 2 May 1883. The range of houses opposite the Clarendon Building was cleared for the New Bodleian Library in 1937.*

Waiting for their grub: crowds attending the ox roast held above Osney Lock in West Oxford to celebrate Queen Victoria's Golden Jubilee in June 1887. The event made a profit of £8 14*s* 6*d*, which was donated to the Radcliffe Infirmary.

Diamond Jubilee gathering in The Square at Eynsham on 23 June 1897. The Freeland Brass Band led the singing of the National Anthem and patriotic songs here before the crowds went off to Mr Webb's field for tea, games and sports.

Mrs S.A. Minns outperforms the other contestants during the Women's Sunlight Washing Competition, held as part of Abingdon's Diamond Jubilee celebrations in June 1897. The event was an unusual feature of the town sports, challenging each woman to wash a dirty cloth in less than three minutes!

Party time in the University Parks on 6 June 1897 as children from the City's elementary schools enjoy all the fun of the fair. They had a good tea as well, drinking 1,400 gallons of tea and eating 21 cwt of cake and 14 cwt of biscuits.

Wantage Market Place on 13 June 1898, when up to 2,000 children and several thousand adults gathered to see the Prince and Princess of Wales drive through on their way from Lockinge to Wantage Road railway station. The man with the top hat, apparently soliciting donations, was the Revd Thomas Houblon, vicar of Wantage.

Coronation dinner for 4,000 people in Chipping Norton Market Square in June 1902. King Edward VII's Coronation was actually postponed at the last minute because of his ill health, but the news came too late to halt this spectacular event.

The boys and girls of Garsington in their Sunday best clothes celebrate the Coronation of Edward VII in August 1902. Henry Taunt, the Oxford photographer, has grouped the boys around the medieval cross and probably did not have too much trouble persuading one of them to perch astride its shaft.

Crowds watch the Coronation procession of decorated vehicles enter Abingdon Market Place on 9 August 1902. In the distance, Mr W. Ackling's float was inspired by an Imperial theme and featured the British Lion, Britannia and John Bull.

Part of the fancy dress procession along Hart Street, Henley, at the time of King Edward VII's Coronation in August 1902. A bicycle disguised as a sedan chair can be seen behind the stalwart figures of the Henley Volunteer Fire Brigade.

Crowds mill around expectantly in Bicester Market Square as the town marks George V's Coronation in June 1911. People gathered here to sing 'God Save the King' at 11.45 a.m. and there was dancing in the Square in the evening.

Happy villagers in the grounds of Longworth House during local celebrations of Coronation Day in June 1911. Sir Clarendon and Lady Hyde hosted a varied programme of events which included dinner, sports, tea, bonfires and a pillow fight.

Some of the children of East Hendred who received special Coronation mugs in June 1911. Many communities also distributed medals and badges which would help to keep alive memories of these occasions.

A child in an MG dress peers happily over the windscreen of a 2-litre drophead coupé MG during an Abingdon parade to mark George V's Silver Jubilee in June 1935.

Hart Street, Henley, *en fête* for the Silver Jubilee in June 1935. Decorations have been strung from every available surface, including the lamp-posts; even the car heading towards the church has a Union Jack on its boot.

An indoor tea party for the boys and girls of the Barton estate in Headington, Oxford, at the time of George V's Silver Jubilee in June 1935.

Boxes serve as impromptu seats and one mum sports a remarkable hat during the Union Street, Jericho, Silver Jubilee tea party in June 1935.

The villagers of Lyneham near Shipton-under-Wychwood celebrate the Coronation of King George VI and Queen Elizabeth on 12 May 1937. The most original fancy dress costume was perhaps the Coronation mug on two legs which required a second mug for the head!

A beautifully turned-out team of horses pulls a decorated waggon through East Hendred as the village celebrates the Coronation in 1937.

'Welcome to Charlbury': cheers ring out in Church Street as local people wave to the Queen and Prince Philip during the Royal visit to Oxfordshire in 1959.

*SECTION SIX*

# PUBS

*Patrons relaxing in the garden of the Swan Inn at Kennington in about 1885. Situated beside the Thames on a piece of land known as Rose, Kennington or St Michael's Island, the pub was a favourite destination for boaters from Oxford and held special events at holiday times to attract extra custom.*

Cheerful drinkers at the George in Botley on 17 August 1892. This was a welcome break for thirsty men who were helping to beat the recently extended boundaries of the City of Oxford.

One for the road in the 1890s: a cyclist fortifies himself with a drink outside the Red Lion in Garsington before mounting his penny-farthing. The barmaid proffers a jug in case he needs a refill.

Arriving in style at the Chequers in Bablockhythe in about 1900 when the landlord was George Preston. A woman sits comfortably beneath her parasol, leaving the hard work to the surprisingly relaxed gentleman on the bicycle in front of her.

Off for the day: members of the Britannia Social Club solemnly prepare to enjoy the fruits of their regular savings, an outing from the Headington pub on 30 July 1904.

Farmers going home from Bampton Horse Fair in August 1904. The Chequers at Brize Norton was the ideal place for a celebratory drink at the end of a successful day.

The King's Arms Hotel at Sandford-on-Thames in 1904. Despite its close proximity to the paper mill, the King's Arms became a popular destination on the river offering meals and billiards as well as 'High Class and Economical Ales for Travellers and Tourists'.

An excursion party in horse-drawn brakes stops for liquid refreshment at the Greyhound on the Faringdon road in Besselsleigh in July 1908.

Welcome to the Hatchet pub in Childrey in about 1910. The landlord, Arthur Froud, his family, a delivery man and possibly several passers-by are persuaded to stand in front of the pub by the photographer, Frederick Ault, in about 1910.

Locals forsake the bar to pose on benches outside the Hare in West Hendred in 1910. The landlady, Mrs Quartermain, is on the extreme left of the group with her husband seated to her left.

Some of the regulars of the Black Lion at Woodcote in about 1920. They were local men working, for the most part, as farm hands or in the building trade; Freddy Tubb, seated centrally on the bench, was known as a jack of all trades who could turn his hand to anything.

*SECTION SEVEN*

# RECREATION

*The Gaitley family orchestra in about 1890: George Gaitley, a former army bandmaster and Oxford resident, poses proudly with his six sons and four daughters who had clearly inherited his musical ability.*

Passers-by in Longwall Street, Oxford, watch Barnum and Bailey's Circus as it processes through the city in October 1898. The circus arrived at Oxford station in four special trains and a mile-long procession helped to attract 21,000 people to its two performances in Abingdon Road.

Members of the Wantage Temperance Fife and Drum Band photographed outside their headquarters, *c.* 1898.

The cinema comes to Witney Feast in September 1900. Beyond the Try Your Strength machine, fairgoers have the choice of the Waroculargraph or A. Ball's Great American Biascope Animated Pictures; entertainments like this would have been most people's introduction to the movies.

The Ickford village band in Sewell's Lane, Sydenham, in about 1900. The band's visit was a feature of Sydenham's annual Club Day on the Wednesday after Whitsun when careful savers received a very welcome payout.

Players in the Souldern village band hover respectfully behind their female supporters in about 1900.

George Mark Morrell tries to look threatening as Captain Hook during amateur theatricals in Headington Hill Hall, Oxford, in 1916.

The cast of 'Robin Hood', residents of Minster Lovell who took their production to Hailey near Witney in about 1920.

Henley Town Band hits the right notes during a concert in the Town Hall, probably between the wars.

The Alfredians or the Woodhill Farm Concert Party at Wantage in 1929. The musicians, from left to right, are Ken Fleetwood, Percy Haig, Howard Crips, B. Phipps, George Taylor and B. Cox.

Children with paper hats, dwarfed by an enormous Christmas tree, take a short break from a party given by the Church Army at Chipping Norton in 1936. The stepladder in the background, next to the four willing helpers, must have been left out after the decorations were finished.

The Six Belles and their accompanying accordionist, Oxford entertainers, photographed in March 1937.

People stop and stare as the Pressed Steel band leads a parade past the Mitre Hotel in High Street, Oxford, in 1952. On the opposite pavement, beside the parked Standard car, there is a glimpse of Long's confectionery shop.

Cheerful French visitors stand outside the Regent Cinema in Chipping Norton in the 1950s. The cinema opened as the New Cinema in 1934 and was later known as the Ritz before being renamed the Regent; it closed down in 1973.

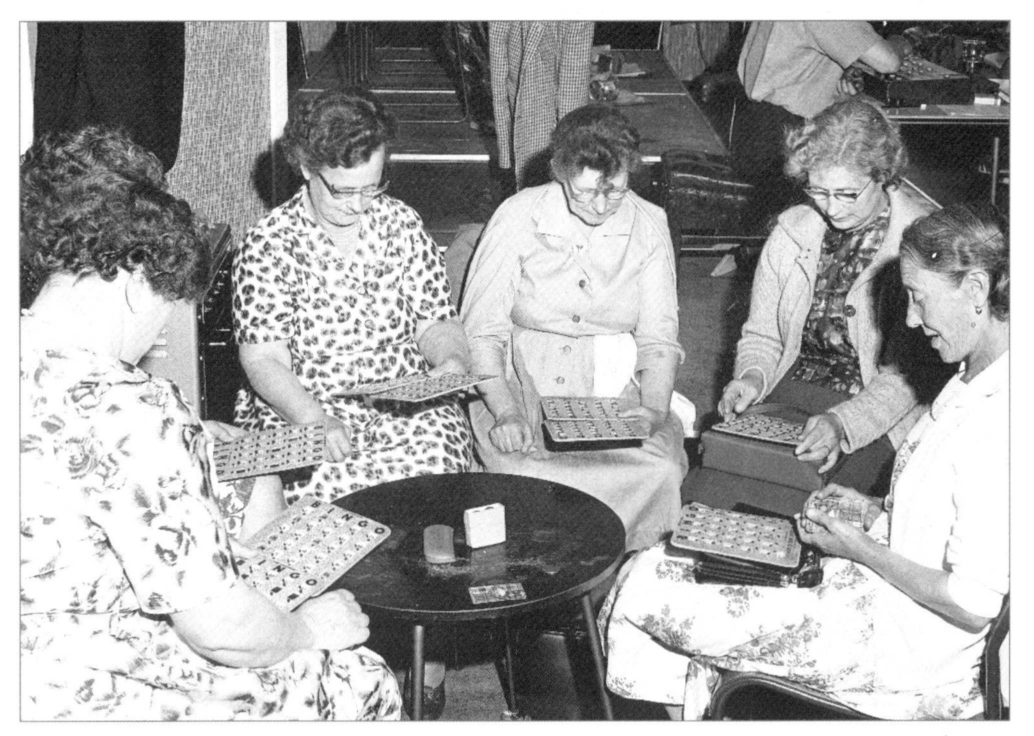

Eyes down for bingo at the Pressed Steel Company's Social Club in Cowley in June 1964. With prize money of over £30 at stake intense concentration was clearly essential.

Teenage girls dance in the background as three judges study the Twist and Shake contest during Pressed Steel's Gala Week in June 1964. The competing local groups at the height of Beatlemania included The Concords, The Ravens, The Planets and The Strangers.

*SECTION EIGHT*

# SPORT

*In the shadow of St Edburg's Church: tennis in the vicarage garden at Bicester in about 1880.*

Members of the Longworth village cricket team in about 1895, photographed in what is now Longworth Manor drive. The team's scorer, James Green, is standing on the left and the village bobby, Frederick James, is standing on the right holding his bat; Percy Sandell (seated left) is wearing dark pads.

Spectators afloat and ashore watch the second heat of the Steward's Challenge Cup at Henley Royal Regatta in 1898. New College, Oxford, beat London Rowing Club by two and a half lengths in this heat but lost to Leander in the final.

A glimpse of Goring and Streatley Regatta near Mrs Telford Simpson's barge in about 1900. This regatta was held each year from 1887 on August Bank Holiday Saturday, and the course extended from the Beetle and Wedge at Moulsford to Cleeve Lock.

Watched with some apparent anxiety by their second, two members of the Margetts family put up their boxing gloves at Watlington in about 1900.

A walking contest in 1904 with Ernest John Clegg, landlord of the Angel at Henley Bridge, hurrying past his pub on his way from Twyford railway bridge to Henley Town Hall. He covered the distance of about 5¼ miles in just 58 minutes 45 seconds.

The opening of Henley Rifle Club's Ovey shooting range at Badgemore on 22 May 1901. Mrs Ovey, the wife of the Club's President, is seated in the foreground and fired the first shot before members competed for three silver spoons which she had presented.

The men and women of Abingdon Hockey Club in the early 1900s. The players are identified as follows, from left to right: A.C. Hyde Parker, -?-, ? Green?, Dolly McCreary, W.E.C. Hutchings, -?- , -?- , May Martin, -?- , Cuthbert Ellison, ? Shawcross, -?-.

A group of boys watch a meet of the Bicester Hunt in comparative safety by standing on the seat around a recently planted tree at Cropredy in the 1900s.

Crowds at the opening of Henley Golf Club in Harpsden on 16 May 1908. All eyes are following the exhibition match between James Braid, the British Open Champion and designer of the eighteen-hole course, and Rowland Jones. Braid began by driving into one of his own bunkers, but he went on to win by 9 and 8.

Slow bicycle race for nurses at Littlemore Hospital at a fund-raising Sports Day held in the 1900s.

Most people remain seated as Henley's roller skating rink is opened for business in about 1910. The popularity of roller skating was short-lived and this building was soon converted into Henley's first Regal Cinema.

An elegant angler waits for a bite on the Upper Thames near Tadpole Bridge in about 1910. Two figures on the eighteenth-century bridge watch with interest, intrigued either by her or by the activities of the photographer.

Women cricketers, apparently mustering two bats and a stump between them, pose with male and female supporters in the Banbury area in about 1910. Women playing cricket in Oxford in 1891 sewed lead shot into the hems of their dresses to avoid accusations of indecency.

Determined athletes at the start of the Stoke Row Marathon, one of the events at the village's annual sports day on August Bank Holiday Monday in 1911. The event was won by O. Flynn with F. Edwards second and J. Everest third.

Headington United footballers in the 1913/14 season when the club won its first county competition, the Junior Shield, by beating the Oxford Institute 5–2 in the final.

The Witney footballers who played the Chipping Norton Workers' Union at Witney in 1914 as a fund-raising event during the lengthy Bliss' Tweed Mill strike.

Defence in depth at Great Rollright as the entire football team poses in the goalmouth in 1924/25. The team came third that season in Division 2 of the Chipping Norton and District League.

The cup-winning darts team from the Swan Hotel at Eynsham in 1925/26. The identified team members are Harry Evans and Mr Howe (back row, sixth and seventh from left), William Evans (middle row, third from left) and 'Little' Billy Betterton (front row, left).

A bowls match is halted for a moment as Mrs A.E. Preston, wife of the Abingdon Bowling Club's President, opens the new pavilion in Albert Park on 6 May 1926.

Swimmers from the Witney and District Swimming Club enjoy the water while others look on; the picture was taken at the old open-air swimming baths on the River Windrush in 1927.

Colin Inns, then twenty-two years old, poses on his bicycle with his boss, W.R. Morris, after winning the 2-mile cycle race at the Morris Motors Sports Day at Cowley in 1932. As a former racing cyclist himself, Morris probably had a special interest in this event.

Spectators stroll and chat during a lull in the racing at Henley Royal Regatta in July 1928. A temporary grandstand is visible across the Thames on the Oxfordshire bank and some of the town's boathouses can be seen nearer the town centre.

Men enjoy an impromptu game of ice hockey on the frozen lake at Chipping Norton during the bitter weather of February 1929.

A shooting party enjoys an *al fresco* lunch in the Wantage area between the wars. The seated men, from left to right, were Ted Belcher, Arthur Belcher, Lieut. Col. John Aldworth, G.W.N. Glover, -?- , -?- , Walter Titcombe. The seated boys were Arthur and Douglas Belcher; Duke Belcher was standing at the back.

Police cyclists battle for the lead at the Oxford City Police Sports Day on the Iffley Road Running Ground in 1936. All competitors had the identical handicap of riding their everyday bikes in full uniform.

Members of the Morris Motors Boxing Club photographed in front of a boxing ring, probably at the company's Sports Day in Cowley in 1937. Lord Nuffield is seated in the middle of the group.

A gliding instructor and his pupil discuss their flight across the opened canopy of a Skylark sailplane at RAF Weston-on-the-Green in the 1960s. A barrage balloon used for parachute training is visible in the background.

Excitement at Ascott-under-Wychwood in September 1963 as the winners of the village wheelbarrow race cross the finishing line well ahead of their nearest rivals.

Watched by spectators on the roof terrace, children lark around at Hinksey Pools, Oxford, in August 1965. This large open-air complex made use of redundant filter beds at the old City Waterworks and opened to the public in 1937.

True British pluck: three women spectators wrap themselves in a rug as a way of surviving the unseasonal weather at Pressed Steel's Sports Day in Cowley in the mid-1960s.

Hounds meet outside the appropriately named Fox Hotel in Chipping Norton on Boxing Day in 1969. A spectator beside the Midland Red bus stop has been forced to lift her poodle up to protect it from an over-enthusiastic foxhound.

*SECTION NINE*

# VARSITY LIFE

*Head of the River in 1886: the determined undergraduates of Magdalen College VIII were, from left to right, G.S. Bazley, W.D Lindley, H. Girdlestone, A.C. MacLachlan, F.P. Bullay, H.F.V. Bull (with dog), J.C.W. Radcliffe (also with dog), W.S. Unwin, H.G.D. Kendall and J.B. Lloyd.*

University Extension students on the steps of Balliol College Hall in 1887. The quartet seated in the front row includes the Master of Balliol, Benjamin Jowett, wearing a mortarboard, and a bare-headed Henry Acland, Regius Professor of Medicine.

Tea on the lawn for women undergraduates at Somerville Hall in about 1895. Beneath the billowing tablecloth, the ingenious wicker tray provided lower-level receptacles for an assortment of cakes.

Archaeologists from the Oxford Architectural and Historical Society at work on the line of the City Wall between the Bodleian Library (right) and the Clarendon Building in 1899. In the background, houses on the corner of Catte Street and New College Lane were being demolished for Hertford's North Quad.

Watched from Radcliffe Square and every available window and balcony, the Encaenia procession, headed by the Chancellor, Viscount Goschen, passes Brasenose College on its way to the Sheldonian Theatre on 22 June 1904.

The exotically costumed members of a children's party held at University College in December 1905.

Taking a dive at Parsons' Pleasure in 1906. Nude bathing remained a feature of this Varsity bathing place on the Cherwell until it was closed in the early 1990s. To spare their blushes, ladies punting on the river were expected to disembark and walk round to the other side of the bathing place!

An enthusiastic crowd on University College barge has a grandstand view of the College VIII during Eights Week in May 1907.

The hardy survivors of the Gridiron Club Ball, still looking remarkably immaculate, pose outside the Town Hall in St Aldate's, Oxford, one early morning in June 1908.

The 'Bees', University College's Second XI, pose outside the college before setting off for a cricket match in Wallingford in 1908. Nostalgic travel by coach and four was all part of the fun and set the tone for a game in which enjoyment was perhaps more important than the result.

Cousins, sisters and aunts pose with related undergraduates in University College during Commem Week in 1909. This sudden feminine invasion was a striking event in a male-dominated University, recalled in Brandon Thomas's play *Charley's Aunt*.

On top of the world: Fred Cripps, an undergraduate at New College in the 1900s, celebrates his arrival by special train for a meet of the Heythrop Hunt at Chipping Norton. His father commented that Fred spent his time at Oxford 'learning how to do nothing gracefully'.

Before the feast: members of an exclusive University College dining club wait for the first of many courses at a dinner in the 1900s.

All eyes follow the ball as the Oxford golfer completes his drive during a Varsity match with Cambridge in about 1910.

Magdalen College beaglers pose in front of the Bell at Standlake in about 1910. They had probably been brought to the village in the horse-drawn vehicles behind the group.

Members of a light-hearted Merton College VIII which achieved nine bumps in races held in about 1912. The crew included J.F. Lambert, A. Dunnage, E.P.O. Preston, W.F. Rogers, H.F. Cartmell-Robinson, J.M. Benson, T.H. Peach, W.K. Reynolds and the cox, W.J. Guthrie.

Glorious confusion on the Isis at Oxford between races during Eights Week in 1913. Crowds from Town and Gown shuffle along the towpath towards Folly Bridge while punters cope with gridlock on the river.

Jesus College undergraduates in very fancy dress pose outside the college sports pavilion during Rag Week in about 1920. The Jack and Jill band occupies the front row of this splendidly bizarre group.

A decidedly masculine 'nursemaid' stops pushing the pram for a moment to show off a very large baby during Jesus College Rag Week in about 1920.

Punts and canoes cause traffic congestion on the Cherwell beside Christ Church Meadow in the early 1920s. Further upstream above the University Parks the river provided much quieter spots for romantic liaisons.

Athletes soar over the wooden hurdles during the University sports at the Iffley Road track in 1937.

Joan Gracey, an undergraduate studying Philosophy, Politics and Economics at Lady Margaret Hall, employs a delicate touch during a tennis match in 1938.

Play up, Queen's! The historian Lord Elton (right) and Charles Henry Gore, Domestic Bursar at Queen's College, watch a cricket match from the college cricket pavilion in Abingdon Road, Oxford, in about 1938.

Lord Nuffield, facing the camera, enjoys tea at St Hugh's College war hospital in about 1945. His companions included J.R.P. O'Brien, Lecturer in Clinical Biochemistry (left) and Robert MacIntosh, Nuffield Professor of Anaesthetics (third from left).

H.R. Bonsey, an undergraduate at University College, snoozes in the sun during the summer of 1908. In his livelier moments, Bonsey rowed for the college and he gained a 4th in Modern History in 1910.